From Crack
to the
Cross

Published by Legacy Press

LegacyPress.org

Your life tells a story; we can help you write it.

©2024 by Reginald D. Watts

All rights reserved. No part of this book may be duplicated or transmitted by any means without written permission from the author.

For permission, please write to rd3000watts@gmail.com

Printed in the United States of America

ISBN (print): 978-1-957026-21-3

ISBN (eBook): 978-1-957026-22-0

Scripture quotations marked (NIV) are taken from the Holy Bible, New International Version®, NIV®. Copyright 1973, 1978, 1984, 2011 by Biblica, Inc.™ Used by permission of Zondervan. All rights reserved worldwide. www.zondervan.com. The "NIV" and "New International Version" are trademarks registered in the United States Patent and Trademark Office by Biblica, Inc.™

Co-authored by Robin Grunder, www.robingrunder.org

Edited by Abbi Beckett, abbibeckettcreatives@gmail.com

Cover design and interior layout by Nelly Murariu @PixBeeDesign.com

From Crack to the Cross

Breaking the Chains of Addiction
and Finding Freedom
Behind Bars

Reginald D. Watts
With Robin Grunder

TO: Sister Ann

Hope You Enjoy this!

R. D. Watt

YHWH

Contents

Foreword   vii

Prologue   ix

PART ONE—Captive in the Darkness   1

Chapter One—A Childhood of Promise   3

Chapter Two—Temptation in the Shadows   9

Chapter Three—Descent into Darkness   15

Chapter Four—Strike One   17

Chapter Five—A Battle with My Demons   21

Chapter Six—Strike Two   23

Chapter Seven—Strike Three   27

Chapter Eight—The Power of Faith   33

PART TWO—Redemption Behind Bars   39

Chapter Nine—Crisis of Faith   41

Chapter Ten—Shadows of Angola   45

Chapter Eleven—Seeds of Transformation   53

Chapter Twelve—Redemption in Study   59

Chapter Thirteen—An Unlikely Connection   65

Chapter Fourteen—Meeting My Football Hero   71

Chapter Fifteen—The Hope of Freedom   79

PART THREE—Embracing Second Chances 83

Chapter Sixteen—The Call 85
Chapter Seventeen—The Heart of Parchman 89
Chapter Eighteen—Prison of Prayer 93
Chapter Nineteen—Love Beyond Bars 97
Chapter Twenty—The Legacy Continues 101

Epilogue 105

Acknowledgements 109
About the Authors 113

Foreword

The first time I met Reginald Watts, he was a prisoner at Angola State Prison. At the time, I was in my twenty-seventh year of full-time prison ministry, and with no stretching of numbers, I had met thousands and thousands of inmates. From the moment we met, I could tell Reginald was different. I immediately recognized something significant about this man—even though he was on the inside as a prisoner at Angola State Penitentiary, prison wasn't inside of him. This significant difference came from his genuine walk with God. Right away, Reginald became my dear brother in the Lord, and for fifteen years solid, we agreed in the spirit that one day he truly would be a free man on the outside. When asked when I thought he would be released from a life sentence, there was only one answer: "Any day now!" I was honored to stand before the pardon board and express my genuine love and respect for a man totally changed and would make a difference in society if given the chance.

My wife and I picked him up when he walked out of the prison that he spent twenty-five years of his life in, and within two hours of driving away from the prison, my cell phone rang with a call from his former Warden, Burl Cain. Out of prison for only two hours and Reginald was asked to become one of the lead chaplains in the State of Mississippi Prison System.

You may ask how something like this can happen or wonder if a miracle like this can happen in your life. You'll find the answer in the pages of this book.

As Iron Sharpens,
Mike Barber, Former NFL football player and Founder of Mike Barber Ministries

> *But my life is worth nothing to me unless I use it for finishing the work assigned me by the Lord Jesus— the work of telling others the Good News about the wonderful grace of God.* (Acts 20:24, NLT)

Prologue

The alley I find myself in is narrow and dark, between towering buildings, barely illuminated by flickering streetlights. The air is heavy with the stench of desperation. Broken glass and debris litter the street, evidence of abandonment. But it's not abandoned . . . this is my area. This is where I belong. This is where I step out of the shadows, briefly, to score and sell. This is also where I'm about to take another hit from the stash I have in my pocket.

But apparently not before I'm found by a dealer I had robbed.

Stealing is not a new thing for me. I've been pulling off robberies with enough success to support my habit, but not enough success to stay out of jail. I was only in jail for a hair less than a year before I was back in again. And the charges I served time for were dropped from armed robbery to simple assault. I served my time in Hattiesburg, Mississippi for eight months, then Jefferson Parish, Louisiana for three and a half months. I was also wanted in New Orleans Parish, but they didn't want me—that's a whole 'nother story. But as for my time being served, yes, maybe I do call that success.

Not the kind of success that you could say jail time did me any good. It wasn't like I learned my lesson, so to speak. Because here I am, about to pull off another robbery, right after I smoke what I've got. It's what I do. It's who I am. Convenience stores, gas stations, people who wanted to buy drugs but did not want to be seen—any place I could get some quick cash. I've also robbed low level street drug dealers and right about now, it looks like that might just catch up to me.

Footsteps echo through my alley, and I know that something ain't right. My heart skips a beat and sweat drips down my face as I turn and see a dealer that I had recently robbed. I'm starting to regret that last robbery. I don't know why I thought I could get away with it, and it was clear to this dealer and his workers that they weren't about to let me get away with it.

I beg for my life as the dealer points his gun at me and the others shout, "Kill him! Kill him!"

"You think you can just walk away after what you did to me, Reggie? It don't work like that. You don't deserve mercy."

I don't want to die, but I know I'm about to as the dealer raises his gun and shoots. Everyone runs. Everyone but me.

I look down at the blood, and I am quivering in pain. Somehow I'm able to get up . . . and smoke that twenty-five cent piece of crack I had in my pocket. I'm in complete physical shock, but instinctively, my actions go to smoking. As I look back on this particular fact, I can't help but think maybe I didn't deserve mercy.

Prologue

I manage to make my way to the corner store on the highway and call the police. "They're shooting! They're shooting! I think a police officer is shot!" I say this knowing that help would come from all directions and a lot quicker than just saying I was shot. I move about half a block in front of a Church's Chicken place and lay on the ground.

Sirens come from every direction. It doesn't take long before two officers find me on the ground. I act like I'm real drowsy 'cause they're asking me questions. They aren't giving me any help, only asking who shot me. One of the officers puts his gloves on and takes his finger and sticks it in the bullet hole to make me talk. I just squirm, and they knew I'm high. Finally, an ambulance comes, and they begin working on me, placing an IV. The officer follows me into the ambulance, but the paramedic puts him out.

The next thing I know, I wake up in the ICU with twenty-five staples in my stomach. The bullet had gone in on the right side of my stomach and made a downward trajectory out of my buttocks. I was amazed at the doctors and nurses. I was twenty-six years old, and everyone believed I was a blessed man to be alive. My mom brought me home a day and a half later, and I was walking with a cane in less than a week.

I wish I could say this was a turning point in my life. Instead, I picked up my cane and decided to go score some more crack.

PART ONE

Captive in the Darkness

Chapter One

A Childhood of Promise

Some of my earliest and best memories that go back as far as I can remember are all about growing up in a tight-knit family in New Orleans, Louisiana. My parents worked hard, loved us unconditionally, and gave appropriate discipline when warranted. There were five of us kids—one older sister, three older brothers, and then me.

My dad owned his own business running dump and garbage trucks. He did just about every kind of job you could with these trucks, but his main gig was a regular route where he picked up trash for the majority of the stores in the biggest mall in New Orleans. It was a lucrative business. He owned three trucks and employed a lot of the dads and older brothers in the neighborhood for periods of time.

He also had a truck that he used to help people move. That was fun because some of the people who were moving would give us kids all sorts of stuff. Having four boys, Dad was never at want for workers. At night Dad would tell us what time we would leave the next morning, and we were sure to be ready.

Unless Mom needed one of us. She would always have the first say. If she was going to do a major house cleaning, she would tell my father which one of us she needed home. If Dad needed us out the door at 6:30, we were up at least forty-five minutes earlier in order to get it together and eat breakfast. If we woke up too late and my father left, Mom would get us up, we would put our shoes on, and wave him down on his way back down the highway.

My dad brought home the bacon, but my mom made sure it was distributed amongst all the bills that needed paying. She was also the spender between the two. She made sure we had food on the table, that all of us kids were well dressed and well groomed. My mother cared about how things looked, and us kids would not be getting away with not taking care of ourselves.

Mom was a Mississippi girl, born and raised, and my dad grew up in southern Mississippi. They met each other down in New Orleans after he got out of the Korean Conflict. Mom was the one who set the tempo of the household. She made all major decisions, and no one ever had a need or a thought to question them.

I grew up in a tight-knit family. I recall playing outside until dark, riding bikes with my brother, Robert. We had just gotten new ones, and we thought they were the greatest bikes in the world. We would ride and ride, even farther than when we used to tag along with the older brothers. Once, we got far enough to where a ramp that was used to roll vehicles up and down onto a train was located. We pushed our bikes up the ramp to turn around and ride back down. When I got to the top, it didn't look the same—it looked two times higher than it did when I was down looking up at it. I remember my brother shooting down the ramp, and there I stood, frozen at the edge. He came back up with me and helped me walk my bike back down. As the youngest of five, my siblings did shelter and protect me in a way. But they also did things like put me up to jumping off the house. All in good, childhood fun.

All of us kids had chores to do, we had an allowance, and we had curfews. We took our turns folding clothes, cleaning the kitchen, cleaning the bathroom, and the basic things that helped us to learn and take responsibility for the household. We were raised to be home before the streetlights came on. If there was any business to take care of, we learned to take care of our issues inside the house and not discuss these things outside. That was just one more thing that added to us being a close family.

Being the youngest in the family did afford me some privileges. I was always taken up for and looked out for by my siblings.

I was four years old when my brother, who is four years older than me, took me to register for school at Paul Lawrence Dunbar Elementary. It was a public school just a couple of blocks away from where we lived. My mama had him bring me in while she was coming from work. I had my birth certificate and all the paperwork, and my brother turned that in. We were told that I was too young to attend public school.

By the time my mama got there and was told that I was too young, she was firm in her response. "How is he too young? He'll be five in January. If he don't go now, he will make his sixth birthday in kindergarten. There's no way I'm gonna wait another year and have him be the oldest student in class."

Mama told my older brother to go to class, and she took me by the hand and walked me out to the car. "I want you to know," she began, "that Mama can do anything, and I'm gonna get you in school." She took me to St. John's Catholic School and registered me for kindergarten. I did end up back at the public school in second grade, but the lesson that Mama instilled in me from that early age was that *nothing is impossible for Mama to do.*

Lo and behold, she lived her entire life that way.

Both of my parents were eighth-grade dropouts. Our education was so important to them that Mama used to say about every other week that everyone in our house was going to graduate from high school and go to college. "Nobody in this house is going to be like your daddy and me," she would say. We all went to great schools, made the grades, some of us played sports, others played musical instruments. We all graduated high school, and all but my oldest sister attended college.

I have very fond memories of high school. There was a lot of football activity that went on in our house. I was a natural at it because I watched it and played it a lot with my three older brothers. I was stronger than I probably looked from all the work I did with my dad and his trash trucks. I went to Warren Easton in New Orleans, which was well known for its academic success. I was also very popular.

My mama always told me that I would be "out front" because I was just born that way. I believe what she meant was that I was a natural leader. And she was right. I was a leader on the football team, I was a leader amongst my peers, and I had a lot of friends who wanted to be around me. I was a leader in just about everything I did, but I didn't always lead correctly.

My parents were not religious folks when I was younger, but they knew God existed, and they wanted us to have a relationship with God even though they didn't. I had and enjoyed what I call a "Leave it to Beaver" life while growing up. There was so much love and respect in our home. I didn't want for anything. Not to say I got everything I wanted, but I had everything I needed and more. I really enjoyed my life.

I graduated high school in 1982 at the age of seventeen. I had absolutely everything going for me. I was raised well.

What I did later on in life had no bearing on the way that I was raised.

Chapter Two

Temptation in the Shadows

I left for Houston, Texas to study petroleum technology at Texas Southern University. It was a new world for me to be six hours away from home and away from my mother, who I had never been away from for more than a day or so. But I had other family members there—my brother who attended and graduated from TSU, a cousin, and later my niece and nephew attended there. We had family members who attended other colleges, but it became somewhat of a Watts family tradition to attend Texas Southern University. The joy I had in my childhood just spilled over into my college life.

I chose to study petroleum technology because that industry was just booming in the '80s. I met a lot of great people. Students from all over the United States and the world, really. During my sophomore year, the homecoming queen was a beautiful Nigerian lady. I remember her speech mostly because of the accent. Coming from New Orleans, you don't hear those different accents. Looking back, I wish I would have lived on campus for a semester or two, but my brother had a two-bedroom apartment, and he was hardly there because of his work in the field of petroleum technology. But I still made friends wherever I went. I'm still friends with a couple of my college classmates today. I thank God for that because by my junior year of college, I ruined most of the friendships I had.

It was my junior year at Texas Southern that I was introduced to a temptation that would alter my life.

Campus seemed to buzz with excitement as some friends and I were getting ready for another wild frat party. I've always been a charismatic presence at events like this. I could laugh and party and have fun just about anywhere I went. As the party went on, I found myself mingling with some new friends that I didn't know all that well. One of them called me over to a corner and asked me if I wanted to try freebasing.

I knew what he was talking about—smoking crack cocaine—but I hesitated. I had experimented with marijuana in the past, but I wasn't sure about this hard stuff. I thought about it briefly. *Could it be that bad if I just tried it at this one party?*

I was led to a dimly lit room filled with smoke and the faint scent of chemicals. I watched as others prepared and smoked from a makeshift freebase pipe with practiced ease. I watched as others lit a flame under the pipe and the powdered cocaine turned into a liquid vapor. When it was my turn, I hesitated only a moment before bringing it to my lips. As I inhaled, the room seemed to shift around me, colors intensified, sounds became distorted, and a wave of euphoria ran through my body. Time lost its meaning, and for that moment, I was transported into a realm of oblivion.

I didn't get hooked immediately. After I first tried smoking crack, I didn't think I would ever do it again until a few weeks later at another party. I liked it. Enough that I would probably do it every other weekend. That turned into every weekend. Days turned into weeks and weeks turned into months as I found myself returning to this drug. What started as an occasional indulgence gradually took hold of me like a vise.

I told myself that I was all right. Even while missing a class or two to use. I started lying to my girlfriend about it. She was already paying my rent. I borrowed money from people I knew and loved, promising to pay them back with no intention of doing so.

Since my dad hauled trash out of the shopping mall, I always had some of the best clothing—items that department stores would throw away because they weren't selling were ours for the wearing. I started selling my clothes and my jewelry. I started shoplifting. I wasn't as well groomed as my mama had taught me to be. When I was nineteen, my mom came to visit me in Texas, and I had lost so much weight that I put on a pair of sweatpants under my jeans in my effort to look okay.

But you can't fool Mom.

She flat-out asked me if I was on drugs, although it came out more like a statement than a question. Of course I lied.

I had two brothers who lived there at the time, and they both knew about it, but they wouldn't dare tell my mom.

Things just got worse and worse. I hooked up with some Colombians. They needed my apartment to make a large transaction outside my apartment door. Our deal was that they would give me two or three hundred dollars' worth of cocaine. They came in and used my phone. I couldn't understand what they were saying because I didn't understand the language. But I didn't care, I just wanted to get them out so I could start smoking my earnings.

One time this dealer wanted a large amount of marijuana. I lied to him and said that I could get as much as he wanted. I had him park in the same spot where previous transactions like this took place, and he gave me a nice bit of cocaine. I acted like I was turning the corner to go to my apartment to get the guy's pot, but I didn't go back to my apartment. I jumped the fence and left with the coke.

It was a couple of days before I returned, and my apartment was torn apart. My brother—who had graduated a couple years prior—came over, looking for me; he didn't know what I had done, but he saw the apartment.

"Man, where you been? I been looking for you," he said.

I told him what happened.

"Do they know you're from New Orleans?" he asked.

I told him no; they didn't have an address or phone number for where I was from. My brother called my mama and sent me home. If I would have stayed, I surely would have been killed. I packed a bag with just a few items and a whole lot of shame, and my brother sent me back to New Orleans.

Without a college degree.

Chapter Three

Descent into Darkness

I wish I could say that moving back to New Orleans with my parents was a turning point for me. But the truth is, I just kept sinking deeper and deeper into my addiction and committing more and more crimes to stay there.

I went to work for my dad, and he fired me four times. I tried to work at other places, but word got out that I could not be trusted. The police started looking for me because I was pulling off robberies. It got to the point where I could not go home in the daytime, and at night, I had to go down the railroad tracks, jump two fences, and go home through my backyard. Every value and moral I grew up learning and living went out the window.

I ran out of friends and family who trusted me. When you are an addict, nothing else matters but the drug. Everything and everyone are second to the addiction. So when my resources ran out, I started doing "snatch and runs" at department stores. I didn't even try to hide my face; I was just thinking about the drug. When people started catching on to who I was, I had to start pulling off nighttime robberies. The drug's grip on me was so tight, and I was stuck in a cycle that I couldn't get out of. If I'm being honest, I didn't want to get out of it.

But my mama never stopped loving me.

One time I called home and Mama answered.

"Darnell," (she often called me by my middle name) "the police been looking for you and you didn't come to the house several times. They parked all around here in different places. The neighbors know about you, everybody knows about you. You need to turn yourself in."

I didn't turn myself in, but soon after that, they picked me up for something. It turned out that they didn't have enough evidence to keep me, so they let me go.

Mom begged me to go to rehab, so I finally did. She picked me up, brought me some clothes, we went out to eat, and then she drove me to a Christian rehabilitation center in southern Mississippi. I stayed there, attended the classes, and graduated the program.

When I was out of rehab, everyone believed that this would be the springboard I needed to get back to being the joy-filled young man that everybody liked and respected.

The young man that I used to be.

Chapter Four

Strike One

After I graduated from the rehab program, I was sent to a halfway house in Hattiesburg, Mississippi, supposedly leaving my mistakes in the past. It didn't take long for me to pick them right back up again.

I now robbed people without shame. I didn't care about anything other than getting my next hit. As my addiction grew, so did the consequences. One such robbery was a cab driver. I hailed him, climbed in the back seat, and once we got where I was going, I took his cash and told him to drive off. I didn't have a gun, but he didn't know that. I really didn't get a good look at his face because I was in the back seat. But he got a good look at me. Two days later he saw me outside of the hotel I was staying at. He called the police.

I got a knock on my door, and I thought it was one of the guys that I was smoking with who also lived in the hotel. I said to come in, but the demanding voice said to open the door—it was the police. They finally pushed the door open and told me I needed to go with them downtown.

"What's wrong officer?" I spoke with a genuine calmness.

"We need you to come downtown."

"Am I under arrest?"

I was told I wasn't under arrest but that I needed to go with them. They put me in a lineup with five or six other men. We each took a turn to stand forward and back and say a few scripted words. The next thing I knew, an announcement came through the speakers, "Congratulations number four, you are under arrest for armed robbery." I was number four in the lineup.

I was sent to the correctional facility in Hattiesburg where I spent eight and a half months going back and forth to court. The cab driver stopped coming to these hearings, so the county attorney offered me a simple assault plea with credit for time served. I was happy with that, but I still wasn't free to go. I was wanted in both Jefferson Parish and Orleans Parish in Louisiana for armed robbery charges in both of those counties. I let my state-appointed lawyer know that I wanted him to call Jefferson Parish first. I had heard that Orleans Parish was known for sitting on cases for a long time. Years even.

Jefferson Parish came and got me from Hattiesburg on the same day I was offered the plea deal. Like I had been told, Jefferson held court pretty fast just like Hattiesburg. I stayed in jail there for three months, and at my hearing, they dropped the armed robbery charges to simple robbery. This charge starts with anything from zero, meaning just probation, to seven years. So they gave me a year sentence, again with credit for the combined time served in both Hattiesburg and Jefferson Parish.

Finally, state officials called Orleans Parish, and Orleans Parish didn't want me. Apparently the prison was so overcrowded, they didn't even want to pursue the case against me. At the time, there were six to seven thousand inmates living in tents and jail cells in Orleans Parish. If I had been sent there before Jefferson, I probably would have sat in jail a year and a half before my case made it to the docket. Jefferson Parish turned me loose, having done eleven and a half months on a one-year sentence.

Both my mom and my girlfriend made sure I always had some money in my account for extra things like canteen and the little luxuries there are in jail. As time drew closer to when I would be released, I stockpiled it, reserving it for the time of my freedom. The first thing I did when I got out was buy some crack cocaine, and I immediately got high.

The first thing I should have done when I got out was go straight home and hug my mama's neck. My family didn't even know I was out of jail until I showed up several days after being released.

I wish I could have seen that entire time and situation for what it was—God working and giving me a chance at a fresh start. But I didn't. In spite of every bad choice I made, my family always stood beside me. My addiction kept me in a state of mind that I had no fear of getting caught because I knew my family would bail me out or bond me out or whatever they could do. And even if they couldn't bond me out, I knew they would still be there for me in whatever ways they could. This line of thinking was all a lie, though, and I was the only one who couldn't see it. I was unrecognizable from the person I was while growing up. I couldn't deny that I was raised well, with values and curfews and discipline—and let me tell you—my mama didn't play when it came to discipline.

And yet, here I was, newly released from prison, on parole, and high.

Chapter Five

A Battle with My Demons

I found refuge in my drugs and my sanctuary in dimly lit streets and alleyways. Night after night the sound of my footsteps bounced against dirty walls as I entered my haven. While taking refuge in my pipe, I didn't hear the footsteps that followed me—until it was too late.

Coming from the shadows, I recognized a dealer that I had robbed. I had also robbed several people who worked for him. Tonight, they all caught up to me, and one of them shot me in the stomach.

I laid there begging for my life. "Please don't kill me! Please don't kill me!"

The gang left, leaving me to die. Even after begging for my life, my first thought was not about how I could help myself. Instead, I reached into my pocket, took out a twenty-five-cent piece of crack, and smoked it. Now I was in shock from being shot—and high as a kite.

The pain was great but bearable after smoking. I figured my time was limited, so I acted as fast as my brain and body would let me. I walked to a corner store on the highway and called 911.

"They're shooting! They're shooting! I think a police is shot!" I thought if I said that last part, help would get to me quicker. I walked another half a block away from where the phone call was made, laid on the ground, and two minutes later, police were coming from all directions. But they didn't notice me at first. When two of the officers finally did pull their car over by me, I acted like I was real drowsy because they were asking me question after question, not giving me any physical help. One of the officers actually put a glove on his hand, took his finger, and stuck it right in the bullet hole.

"Who shot you? What are you high on?" I just kept mumbling until an ambulance came. The officer got in the ambulance with me to ask me more questions, but the paramedic put him out. I was taken to the closest hospital—just two miles away.

The officer followed the ambulance to the hospital and kept peppering me with questions until finally the ER staff put him out. The next thing I remember is waking up in the ICU with twenty-five staples in my stomach. They didn't sew me up.

My vitals after the surgery were good, and it was determined by the doctors, nurses, and my mom that I was a blessed man to even be alive. It took me less than a week to walk with a cane and the same amount of time for me to walk out of the house to score more crack.

I don't know why God let me live only for me to go back to my wicked ways. How many chances would he give me?

Chapter Six

Strike Two

I was blessed to not die in my sins when I got shot, but getting shot didn't make me change any of my ways. I spiraled further into my addiction and continued stealing from people and robbing places. Nothing mattered. Family didn't matter. Sex didn't matter. Staying well groomed and looking nice like I had grown up didn't matter. I became a monster of a person, totally unidentifiable physically, spiritually, and mentally. That caught up to me, and I was once again convicted of two counts of armed robbery and one count of attempted robbery.

They offered me six years on all three counts, so eighteen years.

Thanks to my family, I was able to pay a lawyer. When she came out from the back, she said that I would do my six years on each count running concurrently, credit for time served, and out in three years with good time. The remaining three would be on paper, meaning parole. Since I had already been there for fourteen months, I was out in less than two years from the time I was sentenced. This was a good deal for me and a good deal for the district attorney—it looks good to have a conviction when he runs for office again.

I served this sentence out in Jefferson Parish.

My mama always said I was a leader, and that was true even while I was in jail. Even when I led badly. I ended up becoming the tier guy for my area of prison. Basically, I was the top of the click. I got all the accolades from security and the other inmates. I served the food, so I was able to say who got more, who got less, and who got any extras. I always made sure that everybody had an equal amount. I was the same way when I was in Orleans Parish the first time, too. So when the inmates saw me come back to jail, they wanted me to be their tier rep. They even told the security that.

Jail time was a time for nourishment for me. I'd be recovering from all the drugs and being out on the streets for two to three days at a time with little sleep and no food. I'd wear the same clothes on the street for days at a time. But when I was released, I weighed 223 pounds, had an eighteen-inch neck, and not an ounce of fat on me anywhere. I was probably in the best shape of my life. When people saw me after I got out, I looked like I'd spent the last two years working out at a gym.

I had my size back on me because I'd been locked up with no drugs until I got out. I looked pretty good on the outside, and I tried to play it off like everything was good on the inside. But that didn't last long. Actually, it lasted thirteen days.

Spiritually, I was no better off than when I went in. It took me all of thirteen days after being released for me to start getting high again. I got into a fight with my girlfriend, and I left home.

And never came back.

I went around the corner to find some friends and show them how big I was. I ran into an old friend, and after talking a while, he said, "Man, you wanna smoke something?"

I should have gone back home. I had my mother's car, and I should have got in it and went straight back home. Instead, I walked a little way with him, and I said, "Yeah, man. Yeah." So my friend went and got a rock, and we went in the alley and smoked. When it was gone, I pulled out some money and sent him to get another one. We smoked that. I had just a little money left when I went around the corner, asked a couple of questions, and found another old friend and scored some crack off him. When I went back another time, he gave me something on credit. I went back again, and he said no. Having no money left, I pulled off another robbery. I got away with it, smoked all night, and the next day I pulled off another robbery. This was my cycle.

When I had money in my pocket, I would buy a big piece of crack, break it into little pieces, sell some, and smoke some.

One night I was in my old hunt where I would hustle, and I heard a familiar voice.

"Darnel, boy, come here." It was my mama calling me to her car by my middle name.

"Mama, you can't be out here like this. There's guns in the bushes. Mama, I got dope."

"You got to come home," she said. "Your parole officer said if you turn yourself in, he's not going to violate you on your parole."

"Mama, he's going to violate me, I got dirty urine. Mama, you have to leave."

That's when Mama pointed to the back seat where my girlfriend was sitting and told me that she was pregnant. I walked Mama back to her car.

"Mama, I tell you what. I'll be home tonight, but you got to leave from here."

I lied. I had no intention of going home, even with the news that I was going to be a father. Little did I know that I might not ever make it back home again.

Chapter Seven

Strike Three

You'll sacrifice anything for drugs, and that is exactly what I did. My life, my family; the love, respect, and integrity I once had was at a level zero. I learned nothing from the first two convictions other than that the enemy had control of my life, and for some reason, that didn't seem to bother me.

I had got into it with a guy over a crack deal. He struck me in the head with a foot-long iron pipe, and I started bleeding like a fish. He took off running, and I tried to catch him because he had my dope. He ended up jumping a fence and started knocking on the door and ringing the doorbell of a house in a middle-class neighborhood. I knew the people would call the police once they opened the door, so I turned and walked a couple of miles to another hospital.

I walked into the emergency room, and immediately I was taken in because of all of the blood flowing from my head. They didn't ask me for any ID or credit card, only my name—to which I gave them an erroneous one. The nurse there was very kind, giving me her dinner and praying over me after they stitched me up, and sending me on my way.

I went right back up the same street looking for the guy who struck me.

I didn't find him, but I pulled off a robbery, then another robbery, and then a third robbery. The third robbery would be the last one I ever attempted.

I had my ball cap on and turned it backward because it was bothering the stitches in my forehead. The lady at the register asked if I was alright. I told her to empty the cash register and put some cigarettes in the bag. "No sudden moves." I actually felt bad that I had scared her, and I apologized before taking off. I went back down the same street where I had the fight, scored some more crack, and smoked in the driveway of an abandoned house.

There was another house located behind the one where I was smoking and if the police ever came, everyone there would jump the wooden fence. I hadn't been using in this area before, so when they did pull up, I didn't run. I walked out to the car, and the officer took my hat off. He told the other guy with me, "You can go."

And to me: "Congratulations. You're under arrest. You are who we are looking for. Put your hands behind your back." I did.

As he was patting me down on the car, he turned me around and asked if I had anything on me. I thought for a second and told the officer that I had a straight razor in my right pants leg. When he went down to pull my sweats up on my right leg, I back kicked him in the chest, and he flipped over. I took off around the car and ran up the embankment. I kept slipping because of the morning dew, and he caught up with me and hit me behind my ear with a flapjack. Shots were fired in the air—probably from the group I was with that had scattered, and the officer took cover. I tried to take off again, but with handcuffs on, I didn't get far.

My circle was getting smaller. Somebody was going to kill me. I had already been shot once, and I was coming back to the same areas where I pulled off the robberies in the first place. There were nights that I would have seizures because I wasn't eating. I don't drink, but I would drink some beer or liquor just to come down from smoking two or three days in a row nonstop. I had swindled guys out of their money by giving them fake crack cocaine. All they had to do was come back to me in a different vehicle, one I didn't recognize, and I would be shot. I had seen it happen to two of my friends. It was only a matter of time before my time would run out.

Apparently when I left the last Shell station that I robbed, a guy and his wife that I had smoked with saw me come out. That information, along with the stitches in my forehead that identified me, was all it took for the police to find me and know that I was who they were looking for. It was only forty-eight days after I was released from Jefferson Parish.

During questioning they held up a picture of a guy that I knew, but I said that I didn't.

"Well he knows you," they said to me. "And he's working with the state to get a reduced sentence on distribution." This guy was a habitual offender on drug charges.

"You know what," I said, "Yeah, I know him. That's my charge. You don't need his testimony. Let him do his time too." I was angry that this guy had turned me in. It wasn't going to make any difference in my sentencing because they had me dead on. But I wanted this guy to do his time, too.

I signed the paper. They booked me.

Strike three.

In just forty-eight days, I had gone from 223 to 159 pounds.

When I left Jefferson Parish forty-eight days prior, I was only out on paper. That means I still had three years of parole. Since I violated those charges and then some, they didn't need to sentence me right away. I was considered a state inmate already, so violated parole is like having a conviction. They shipped me to the Department of Corrections and then to Allen Correctional Center in Louisiana where I did thirteen months before bringing me back to Jefferson Parish for sentencing. I was trying to get the charges dropped to simple robbery, but the District Attorney told my lawyer and my mom that they were going to take me to trial because there was no way I would stop robbing.

I looked at my mama and told her not to pay any more lawyers. I was going to ride this one off. I asked for a twenty-five-year sentence thinking I would do half that time and maybe even earn a year for good time. I didn't want to go to trial.

The DA said no.

I asked my lawyer to plea for thirty-five years.

Again, the DA said no. They were going to take me to trial and insist on a life sentence.

Chapter Eight

The Power of Faith

While I was waiting for a court date for trial, I fell right back into some of the leadership roles I had before when I was in. Again, I became the tier rep or spokesperson for the tier in jail. I would rack my door back and forth at night, and they would let me out. I would make some money or some trades by selling little snack pies and bringing a light to other inmates on my tier. As the tier rep, I had the lighter all the time, so I'd give a light to a dude for a bag of potato chips. They could get two lights for a pack of cookies.

I had the security officer timed when I was giving lights and making these trades, so when he was on my side of the dormitory, I knew he would go back to the booth and then leave to go do his rounds on the other side. He would be gone for fifteen to twenty minutes. This is when I would "sell" some lights to people. Then I would return to my cell before he returned.

One night I wasn't fast enough. Corporal Paul, one of the meanest little men there, asked me what I was doing out. I said I was just hollering at one of my guys. We weren't supposed to be talking at this time, so they brought a chain and took me to a lockdown dorm. There was nothing but a toilet, a bed, and a feed port.

And a Gideon Bible.

I opened it up and started reading something in Romans about doing things I don't want to do and not doing the things I do want to do. Further down it said something about how it's no longer me, but the sin that lives in me.

I got offended at God when I read that. I didn't want to be a weak man. If I didn't want to do something, then I should be strong enough to not do it. I read it again. Something about being a broken and torn man resonated with me. The author said that nothing or no one can deliver me from this state but Jesus Christ.

I read it a few times before I closed the Bible and closed my eyes. I didn't sleep well, and I just felt unsettled in the morning. I didn't know at the time that this was the Holy Spirit working in me.

I grabbed the Bible again and when I opened it, it fell to Romans on the exact page I had read the night before. I don't know if that page was wrinkled or puffy and that's why it opened up there, but it did. So I read it again, and every word stuck with me. I was not as angry or offended as I was the night before. I was relating to the author of this passage, and something was happening inside of me.

I didn't get saved that day, but I could quote Romans 7:14-25 word for word, and something changed in me.

I do not understand what I do. For what I want to do I do not do, but what I hate I do. And if I do what I do not want to do, I agree that the law is good. As it is, it is no longer I myself who do it, but it is sin living in me. For I know that good itself does not dwell in me, that is, in my sinful nature. For I have the desire to do what is good, but I cannot carry it out. Now if I do what I do not want to do, it is no longer I who do it, but it is sin living in me that does it. So I find this law at work: Although I want to do good, evil is right there with me. For in my inner being I delight in God's law; but I see another law at work in me, waging war against the law of my mind and making me a prisoner of the law of sin at work within me. (Romans 7:15-23, NIV)

I resonated with words like "law" and "prisoner." I've been breaking the law for nearly a decade now. I've been in and out of jail and prison for about half of that time. I never set out to be an addict. I never imagined while I was growing up that I would be sitting where I was sitting that day—in a cell, waiting to find out if I was going to be in prison for the rest of my life.

From that morning in my cell on, I no longer wanted to smoke crack. I wanted to go home and have a real job and pay my bills. I wanted my family to be proud of me. I wanted to be the father to my child that I should be.

Not long after that night alone with the Gideon Bible in my cell, I gave my life to Jesus, and I never looked back. And when I say I got saved, I got *saved*. There was no more getting high. I thanked God every day for His mercy, knowing that I didn't deserve it. I started reading my Bible every day and sharing what I was learning and reading with other inmates. I led Bible studies in prison and preached at one of the inmate-led churches.

My mother came to visit me often while I was awaiting trial. On one of those visits, I told her that I was saved. She said she believed it now. "Before you was trying on your own. You had the language of being saved, but you wasn't. Now you saved. You don't ask for the same things; your language has changed. You're back to the son that I knew." My mama never minced words when I was growing up, and she wasn't about to start while I was in prison.

She also never abandoned me. I was never without her other than the times I was on the run. And even then, I could call her, and she would meet me somewhere.

I think the worst of it became the best of it—*crack cocaine led to my salvation.*

For the first time in all of my court dates, I didn't tell my mama when trial was set. I didn't want her there. Not because she wasn't supportive of me, and not because I didn't want to see her. I was ashamed, and I didn't want her to see me. I didn't want her to hear all of the horrible things I was guilty of. So when I was escorted into the courtroom and sat beside my lawyer, I was surprised to hear a familiar voice come from behind me: "Hey baby." I looked over my shoulder and there sat my mama and my pregnant girlfriend.

The trial did not last long because I wasn't pleading "not guilty." I did, in fact, rob the place, and I deserved time for that. But I was pleading guilty to a lesser charge than armed robbery because I did not have a gun. I gave the impression that I had a gun, but I didn't have one.

I'll never forget the look on my mother's face and the sound that she made when they played the video of me robbing the store and running out the door with the money. That sound still haunts me from time to time.

The jury deliberated for all of thirty minutes.

Guilty.

They gave me a twenty-five-year sentence and vacated that because I was a habitual offender. My sentence: L-I-F-E. There were no numbers attached, which meant I would never be given parole. I would never be a free man.

I wasn't expecting my sentence to go this way. I knew in my heart I was a changed man, and I truly thought that God would want me to see freedom.

But I still had hope. I had been a slave to my sin, and it was my sin that put me here. But I was no longer a slave to that sin, and I committed to operating my life in the freedom of Christ—even as a prisoner in the state of Louisiana.

PART TWO

Redemption Behind Bars

PART TWO

Redemption Behind Bars

Chapter Nine

Crisis of Faith

Very early on in serving a life sentence, I was able to get past a lot of things, thanks to God. I was able to look beyond my past of being a former crack addict, of hurting my mother and father and siblings, and for not being there for my only child. I could only do this by leaving that stuff at the foot of the cross because honestly, it was just too much for me. Each time I laid my burdens and shame down, God showed me that He had me, and He cared for me. He had to pull me out of the wreckage that I had gotten myself into. This was the hope I held on to.

And after all the work that God had done in my life, even while in prison, I nearly threw it all away.

I was in my cell when I got news that shook my entire world. The chaplain came in and said we needed to talk. I could see the heaviness in his eyes and hear it in his voice.

"Reggie, I got some bad news. There is no easy way to tell you this, but your mama died last night."

"Oh, Chap. Come on, man."

The chaplain walked me to his office. I talked with my family on the phone there. I didn't want to believe this was true, and I argued with my family. I argued with God. There was nothing that anyone could tell me. I wanted

Mama to come back. I didn't want to live in a world that my mama was no longer in.

I went back to the dormitory and told the guys there to leave me alone. I told them not to talk to me and not to get near me. If they did, I would kill them.

I did this for two or three days before an old man named Diamond walked up to me. He said, "You preaching and teaching Bible study in here, you need to live by that word."

"Get away from my bed!" I shouted.

He balled his fist up, and he stepped back a little bit. "I'm not scared of you. You need to practice what you preach."

"Get from my bed now!" Everyone around was looking, but no one was going to come near me because they didn't know what I would do. I didn't even know what I would do.

So Diamond says again, "Man, you need to get back to what you was over there teaching. You got us sitting at the table telling us what to do. Now it's time for you to do it, and you just want us to stay away." He looked at me one more time and walked away slowly with his back to me.

I started crying. Every single one of them done saw me cry so many times over the past few days. This time I cried out to God.

"I don't want to live. But if you give me the strength to want to live, I'll live for you the rest of my life." That was my cry. That was my prayer.

I felt a calm. I don't know if it was instant, five minutes later, five hours, or five days . . . I don't know. But it was such a calm that came over me that I knew it was the Holy Spirit. I didn't know how to dissect it or move in it. I didn't know if it was going to stay in me or around me or if I would have to ask God for it every moment of every day. But I do know that God came to me at a time when if He didn't come, I don't know what I would have done. I really don't know. If that old man had been a younger man, we would have been fighting. Win, lose, or draw would not have mattered. I just wanted somebody to take me out. That's how sickening the situation was to me. And that's how I knew it was God that came to me.

My mom's passing was the most devastating thing that has ever happened in my life. I had never had anyone so close to me die before that, so I had no measuring stick or way of knowing how to deal with it.

But God heard my cry, and He answered. I stayed true to my word to live for Him.

Chapter Ten

Shadows of Angola

Angola State Penitentiary was known as the bloodiest prison in the United States. When I got to Angola in 1998, it was nothing to see a man on the floor at three or four o'clock in the morning on your way to the bathroom, just lying in a pool of his own blood. There was one security officer overseeing a dorm of sixty-eight men, and he would act like he didn't see anything, hoping that the shift would change, and he wouldn't have to do the paperwork.

Men in prison didn't do much talking or figuring things out. It was more like you had to get information to work with before you could get anything. I learned early on that I was considered an inmate amongst the prisoners and the security. An inmate is someone who doesn't know the rules of prison. They don't know the game or what's going on. He thinks that if he sits on his bed and keeps to himself that he's not going to be messed with. But quiet only draws more attention, especially when you first come into a zone or dormitory. When you get there and put your stuff by your bed and just sit looking forward, guys are watching you and talking about you for the next thirty-six to forty-eight hours. They're not going to wait long because there may be guys that come in from another dormitory who heard that there's a weak one in yours.

If you are seen as weak, a convict will come into the showers and turn a weak inmate into a woman. Then the convict will sell the man to others for four or five hundred dollars. As far as prison terms go, an inmate can remain an inmate forever, or for as long as it takes to not be seen as weak.

A convict, on the other hand, is a guy who knows the rules of the game. Before a convict makes a move on an inmate, he will allow his victim to make some sort of move of his own. The convict might be hanging out in the TV room, watching, and waiting to start a conversation with a perceived inmate. He might say, "I don't know where you're from, but I'm from . . ." Convicts will try to make nice conversation, but it's a lie. No conversation is ever really nice.

But the inmate doesn't know that, so he thinks that the convict is being friendly. So the youngster will open up and say, "I'm from . . ." and then ask where the convict is from.

That's a big red flag. In prison, nobody ever asks another man where he's from unless he was planning to pull something off.

But if the convict can get the inmate to start talking, that's exactly where they want the younger, weaker man. If something like women's lingerie comes on TV, the convict will try and see where the inmate is sexually drawn. That's another bad thing about prison . . . even if you are heterosexual, the convict just wants to know, because if you are, they will send a homosexual at you. The convict will try and bait the new inmate by giving him something he wants like oral sex, and then turn around and say, "Now you got to do me." The new guy doesn't understand, and that's when the knives come out. The two are in a secluded area, and the guy who had been talking to the inmate is watching the whole thing. The inmate is now his man. If he doesn't obey, then there are two knives facing him.

I have rescued a few of these guys, and only one time did I regret it. The man I thought I was helping get out of this horrific situation continued to hang around the people he kept company with. He took some drugs that they offered him and eventually ended up owing money. He couldn't pay his debt except for giving himself up as trade. The convicts knew exactly what they were doing.

There weren't gangs in Angola, but wickedness, evil, and violence ran rampant. The convicts outnumbered the inmates. The guy that stands alone is outnumbered. But I will tell you this—if you stand alone, the convicts will give you a fair shake. If you remain a man and let them know no matter how many times they beat you, you'll never do the vile things they want you to do, you'll earn respect. You might get a couple of guys sent at you, get a busted lip or something, but you won't have to face the wall while you shower or go with the man who told you to carry his clothes and yours.

I was walking with a friend, whom I had met early in my days at Angola, from a church service 'to the TV room. This is the first room in the dormitory. We wanted to watch Stone Cold Steve Austin wrestling the Undertaker. I was rooting for Stone Cold. Another man came up to me. "You braggin' on Stone Cold, Watts? You wanna put some money on it? 'Cause I like the Undertaker about $20 worth." I didn't want to gamble on the match. Not that I didn't put money down on things, I did gamble with football and football tickets. But he seemed alright with it.

When the match was over, we walked to the back, and there was fighting all over the dormitory. People were really going at it.

"What we done walk into?" I asked the man who wanted to bet on the wrestling match.

It turned out to be New Orleans inmates against Baton Rouge. One guy that I was helping tutor to get his G.E.D. was coming by with the bottom of a push broom. I took it from him. He was from Baton Rouge, but I would have taken it even if he was somebody from New Orleans.

It just so happens that there is no such thing as "it just so happens." God had placed me there at the right time, and I had no fear about getting involved to try and stop the fight. There were sixty-eight men in the dorm, and about seventeen or eighteen were fighting. A guy came at me with locks in his belt. I took it from him, and when he turned around and saw me, he didn't want to fight anymore. Then there were two-on-one in the fight in front of me, so I pulled one of the dudes off and told the other two to go ahead and fight. I turned the other dude around, and I don't know what got into me. I wasn't fearful, or mad, or upset. There is no emotion that I can recall.

Finally the security officer came and said if everyone stopped fighting, that he wouldn't call the ranking officer. I thought that was crazy. People are bleeding all over the place, and he was the security officer.

Things started to cool down, and extra security came in. Everyone was told to sit on their bed, and everyone's hands were checked to see who was fighting. Joe, the man who slept across from me, whispered, "So you think you can break up a fight like that? Who you think you are now?"

"Who going to stop me from breaking it up?" I got a little loud, and he thought I was crazy.

We all had to go to the TV room and line up on the benches while our dorms were searched. They found some knives and took another guy out. We were allowed to go back to our beds, but there was word that this wasn't over. Me and one other man took turns keeping watch all night.

I started getting more respect from convicts and inmates on any side of the argument. Word even got to my brother who lived in Texas.

There were three prisoners who had been in for murder. They were juveniles when they went in and were found innocent after twenty-eight years. They were in Texas outside of an eating establishment, and they were talking about Angola. My brother heard them and asked if any of them knew Pastor Watts. One of them said, "Yeah, I know Reginald. Man, he was my pastor." They went on to tell my brother that I could go into any dormitory in any camp, and if something was going on that wasn't supposed to be and I said something, it stopped. They told my brother about a time when two of the worst guys in prison were getting ready to jug each other up, and I walked in, talked to them, and nothing happened. "I've never seen anyone be able to do something like that in Angola."

Angola was known as the bloodiest prison in America for good reason. At least half the guys in my dormitory had some sort of weapon. It was just bloodshed up and down the halls, on the basketball court, in the weight room, in the dormitory, in the bathroom, in the shower, in the kitchen . . . everywhere. I have seen security officers get their heads busted. There were more fatalities, more stabbings, more bloodshed, and more guys getting hit over the head with bricks and locks than in any other prison. It went on for years.

Angola was just a godless place. Satan was running rampant.

But the Holy Spirit was working. It may not have been as prominent, but God is far more powerful. And I got to see just how powerful my God is, even in the bloodiest prison in America.

Chapter Eleven

Seeds of Transformation

Every camp at Louisiana State Penitentiary in Angola has its own inmate-led church with several churches that operate within those chapels. The main prison has four churches which are twice as big as any chapel in the camps. There is the hospice chapel, the Catholic chapels, the Tutti Chapel, and the interfaith chapel that is typically attended by Muslims and other denominations.

Inmates and a board of directors would vote on who would lead each church. Eight months into my life sentence at Angola, I was voted in to be the pastor at a church in Camp C where I lived.

I did not volunteer to be included in this vote. I didn't think I could be a pastor. I was content just leading Bible study in the parish. When I found out about the vote, I said no.

"Man, we voted you in," one of the inmates told me. "Tell you what you do—sleep on it. Talk to God. See what He say."

I already knew the answer. I knew when I learned about the vote. I was just holding back, which I promised

God I would not do. Eight months after I became an inmate at Angola, I became a pastor of a church at Angola.

The guy who was the previous pastor in Camp C taught me so much, especially about what to do and some of what not to do. I was well studied in the Word, and I was capable of leading men. Like I said before, I've always been a leader. In those early days of pastoring, God surrounded me with guys who were more spiritually mature than I was, but willing to sit under my leadership. That was special.

I grew in my walk with Christ, and the congregation grew right along with me. The numbers grew in a way that people in high places took notice—including the head warden of the prison, Warden Cain.

"Chaplain Watts," he told me, "This is one of the strongest churches in this prison. I like this church." That meant a lot because Warden Cain had to go to all of the prison churches.

What was it that made the church that I pastored so strong? I don't know. I didn't know what a strong church was, and I didn't know what a weak church was. All I knew was how to love people. So that is what I did. I loved people, met them where they were at, and pointed people to Christ.

The love and leadership part came easy, that is just who I am. But being a pastor in prison has a lot of challenges. My congregation didn't consist of people who dressed in their Sunday best and showed up to church full of niceties for everyone around them. My congregation consisted of some of the worst of the worst of convicted felons. Their language and behavior in church was not always befitting of your typical church congregation. Not only was I leading the inmates, but I lived with them. I got to see how they lived in the dormitories, on the basketball court, in the kitchen . . . I got to see their true colors. We didn't just talk about sin, we talked about living in sin. I had a lot of people who didn't want to give up living in their sin.

None of that mattered. I was anointed to be a pastor, and I pastored the only way I knew how—with love.

Even the worst of the worst can change. I've seen that firsthand in a guy named Chili Red.

Chili Red had killed three or four people while in prison in Angola. He stabbed a couple of security officers. He used to take the light bulbs out of the cell, and when a security officer came by, he threw the long fluorescent bulbs, hitting them upside the head. He did all kinds of things like that. He lived in Camp J—a lockdown for the worst of the worst—until they moved him over to Camp C with me. His reputation preceded him. Everyone knew who Chili Red was.

Apparently my reputation as a senior pastor in Camp C was known in his camp as well.

"You Pastor Watts?" he asked. "I heard about you when I was at Camp J. Man, they just pulled me back here a couple days ago. I don't know how long I can stay in population." Chili went on to tell me how he knew he couldn't live around people because he knew he would hurt somebody.

"I know your reputation," I said to Chili. "You can live in this camp 'cause you can get away from people. If you find that you don't want to be in this dormitory, I can get you moved to another, or even the other side of the compound. But I think it best if you stay in this dorm." I believed that there was a reason God had placed Chili in Camp C, and I believed there was a reason that Chili came to me.

Unfortunately, I didn't see that reason right away. A couple of weeks after he moved to my dormitory, a guy who had had problems with Chili in the past jumped him and hit him in the head with locks. They locked that guy up and moved Chili.

I know seeds were planted in the short time I had with Chili Red. He would write me long letters and ask me to help him get some of his enemies out of his prison records. He didn't want to get into more trouble. I didn't have that kind of pull, but I continued to write and keep tabs on Chili, and I knew he was sincere in reaching out to me.

As years went by, I heard about some times that Chili did get into more trouble. One of the wardens in Chili's camp was doing shakedown. Shakedown is when an officer has to go in and beat you up when you act up, and this warden had to shakedown with Chili. But later on, this same warden told me that Chili didn't get into trouble anymore and that he would be the first person to help Chili out if he needed it. Years passed before I heard this news, but it was exactly what I needed to hear.

God gave me more confirmation that I was right where I needed to be, doing the work He needed me to do, showing me that even the worst of the worst can change.

Chapter Twelve

Redemption in Study

Warden Cain was a visionary when it came to offering opportunities for betterment for the inmates at Angola. He believed in providing self-help programs, fostering healthy community within the prison camps, and opportunities for study. These were opportunities that most of the prison population may never have had, inside or out of prison. One of the programs that I took advantage of was Bible College.

Classes for Bible college were offered in a four-year cycle. Every four years, the classes would start over at freshman-level courses, then sophomore, and so forth. If guys were interested in taking Bible college courses, they would jump in at whatever year they were teaching. Professors would come in from New Orleans, community colleges, and other colleges to teach. Sometimes that meant that guys would begin with the junior or senior-level classes, then rotate back around to the freshman classes, and then graduate after sophomore year. If you were to miss a semester, you had to wait another four years for those same classes to come back around. In 2013, I was fortunate to get in on the cycle from the beginning and graduate with a seminary degree four years later. But for one week during those four years, it looked like I might not make it through a semester. I missed eight days of classes because they threw me in the dungeon for something I didn't do.

Every Sunday in October and the third weekend in April, Angola had a rodeo. I was allowed to sell my woodworking hobby craft during the rodeo. My specialty was handmade rocking chairs. Each year I would order the materials I needed from Pat's Hardware Store. One year I placed my order, and they messed it up. It was getting close to rodeo time, so I kept that order to begin working, but when my second order came, it wasn't mine. The wood was bad. So I wrote to the wood company, and they said they would replace it, so I sent that second order back.

A lady that I had done some other woodworking for had ordered forty-eight rocking chairs from me, to be sold and picked up at the rodeo. I wasn't able to meet that order due to the order with the hardware store being messed up and then the wood being poor quality. When the proper materials were finally delivered, the rodeo had already passed for the year. I made an arrangement with the lady who placed the order to have her pick them up at the front gate. When she came asking for them, the guards said that it wasn't allowed. She got all up in arms, saying she was going to call her senator and state representative and whoever she had to and tell them about the situation. The guards didn't like that, so they called back to my camp and said to send the rocking chairs to the main gate, but I was not allowed to take them. She wrote a check to me, and it went into my account through the inmate banking system. What she didn't know, and I didn't think of at the time, was that this was going to backfire on me.

At the rodeo, taxes are charged and taken and paid from my income. When a check was made out to me and went through the inmate banking system, it looked like I was trying to get away with not paying taxes. It ended up being a huge deal, and they were threatening to lock me up in the dungeon. I had to tell them to take the taxes out because I wasn't trying to get away with anything. It was all documented. I had written the head of the rodeo, I wrote to the warden, I spoke or wrote to everyone that I needed to about the situation with the lumber and my order being wrong and then late. It was chaos, but they didn't lock me up.

That time.

Two years later I made one rocking chair for a guy who had a son in prison. Everything was all legal, I had the paperwork signed and everything approved. But I couldn't sell it to the man, I had to give it to him. That was normal, and I was not expecting any payment.

When the man came to pick up his chair, he put eighty dollars into my account, twenty of which he asked me to give to his son for canteen. His son was in the work cell block and not able to get to canteen himself.

I was sitting in my Bible class when someone came and got me.

"I got to take you to the office. They want to lock you up. What did you do?"

"What? I didn't do anything!"

The guard went on to say, "You sent a rocking chair to the front gate. You gotta pack your stuff. I gotta lock you up."

I had the paperwork in my dormitory. I wasn't trying to sell the rocking chair. I had no idea the guy I gave it to was trying to get his son money through me.

They walked me down to cell nine. Out of the first eight cells, seven people knew me. Each cell had two people. When they saw me get locked up, they took it as a statement that if they were locking the pastor up, they surely would never get out of the dungeon.

The free man on that block came up to me and let me and the guy in the cell with me out so I could talk to everybody up and down that cell block. I told them what I was in for and took the opportunity to pray with everybody. I stood back and prayed as loud as I could so everyone could hear.

Later when they released me from the dungeon and I was back in Camp C, I got a letter from one of the most viscous guys that was on the dungeon block with me. They called him King Kong, that's how wild he was. But I never had a problem with him.

"You being here kind of gives me hope. I don't want anything to happen to you or me. It's time for me to do the right thing. I want to be around you when I get out. Don't forget about me."

I stayed in the dungeon for eight days before they let me out. The warden was the one who came to my defense and had everything taken care of. But because I had missed so many classes in a row, they threatened to make me drop out. If I wanted to re-enroll, I would have to wait another four years for that semester to roll back around.

One of the professors called the warden on my behalf.

"Sir, we have a student, one of my pastors, and I need him in class. Whatever he done, he's going to make it right, he's going to offer burnt offerings, and he's never going to do it again." He said this in front of the whole class.

I was allowed to stay in class and complete my schooling in four years. The favor of God was everywhere I turned. Even here at Louisiana State Penitentiary in Angola.

Chapter Thirteen

An Unlikely Connection

Selling my woodworking and leather craft was how I made money when I was in prison. The rodeo was always a great place to connect and sell what I was making, but that only took place twice a year. The rest of the time I had to depend on friends and family in and outside of prison to help me out. I can't begin to tell you how many times I had been burned by my loved ones on the outside thinking they would sell my hobby craft and reimburse me, only to take what I had and take the money right along with it. My friend, Barbara, was one of the biggest supporters of my hobby craft, and she helped me make sales.

Barbara was a police officer, a juvenile detective, and she oversaw a prison ministry at the church she attended. I met Barbara through a mutual friend who she would come to visit. This man also helped me make connections and sell my craft, but when he mentioned that his friend Barbara might also be able to help, I was skeptical. But my friend made the introduction one day while she was visiting. I was working the visiting shed at the time, making sure visitors and their inmates had food, and I was always there to pray with whoever asked. Sometimes inmates would invite me over to their table to show their visitors that they had someone who was a good influence on their side while on the inside. I was there for them and their visitors.

I met with Barbara on several occasions while she was visiting a friend she had grown up with. When the topic of my hobby craft came up, I had a list given to me from our mutual friend, and he told me to give it to her. She was more than happy to help me out. I told her what I wanted for each item I made.

"Don't you think your price is a little low?" she asked as she looked the list over.

"I sell more this way than if I try to inch up my prices. I want to give you a percentage."

"I have all I need out here," she would tell me.

She wouldn't take anything for helping me out. Not a percentage, not a quarter or dime. She always came back to me with the exact amount that I had priced my items at and never took even a nickel for herself.

We worked like this for a number of years. She would help me fill in the gaps in selling my craft. We would also visit every time she came to the prison—whether she was taking juveniles on tours as a part of her prison ministry work, visiting friends she knew, or visiting me. She would also bring some of her family members along to visit with me. I got to know her aunt, her children, and her grandchildren quite well over the years, both through prison visits and at the rodeo.

Being involved in law enforcement, Barbara brought a unique perspective to our visiting table. For ten years, I would look across the table and see a good friend who is also a juvenile detective and a police officer. And by all accounts, I imagined when she looked across the table at me, she must have seen a menace to society. Someone like me was a person she would have to correct or arrest if I was on the outside. My very best friend was someone I would have run away from had it been ten years prior and I was a free man. If I ever had any question about whether or not I was a changed person, I didn't anymore. The things that I once counted as my enemy, or counted as not being good for me, became the very same things that nourished my soul. My friendship with Barbara nourished my soul.

We held the very same views on the things that mattered, but from different sides of the table. She learned hers early. She listened to her mother. I learned mine late because I disobeyed my mother. I had to learn my lesson—my faith—in prison. But we both ended up on the same road, in the same book, and on the same page, but from two opposite perspectives.

Barbara became more than my best friend. I fell in love with her, but I was afraid to tell her. I couldn't see any reason why she would want to be involved as anything more than a friend with someone who was serving a life sentence without the chance for parole. I was afraid if I told her, it would ruin our friendship. Maybe she would tell me that she didn't mind being my friend or helping me with my hobby. All of these things raced through my mind until 2017, ten years after we met, when I told her about my feelings.

"Look, I need to talk to you." I waited until the end of our visit out at the visitor's shed before telling her I was in love with her.

She was speechless. Without saying another word, we hugged, and she left. Our visiting time was over. After every visit she made, I would always call her to make sure she made it home. This time I was hesitant. I was afraid of what she would say. But I called anyway.

"We'll see where this goes," she told me on the phone.

To me, this was a yes. She left that door open just a little bit, so I no longer needed a crowbar to open it. I had an inch. I wasn't about to pull the door all the way open, but little by little over the next handful of years, we got to know each other on a new level. We loved each other as more than friends—as a couple.

Her mother, Margaret, became my mother, and she would pray for me every day. I called her often from prison, and on one of our calls she laid some things out there.

"Baby, don't lose hope. Don't give up. Don't lose faith 'cause you coming out of there. I told God 'enough is enough' and He got to let you out of there."

It's not that I never had hope that one day I would get out of prison. But it was hard to see as I had no pardon waiting for me, no parole, or even a hearing to determine if I could get parole. Her response blew me away.

"You getting out of prison. It's not for you to say how, that's up to God. So start saying it and believing it. You getting out."

This statement changed my whole perspective—not on just getting out of prison, but a whole lot of things. Deep, deep down, I did believe that I would someday get out. That God would make the impossible possible. But on the other hand, I knew He had me inside this prison for a reason. I was ministering to people that needed God. I was able to do it in ways that no one from the outside would ever be able to. I was not only leading these men—some of them the worst of the worst—towards Christ, but I was walking alongside them day after day. Truly this is what discipleship is all about. There was no doubt that God had me exactly where I belonged.

But the desire to be a free man was always there. And it wasn't for me to tell God if, when, or how.

Chapter Fourteen

Meeting My Football Hero

Football has always been a love of mine for as long as I can remember. I grew up in the pre-cable days, so as a kid, we only had football games on television three times a week—college on Saturday, pro ball on Sunday, and a Monday night football game.

Football was something that I had in common with the brother who is closest to me in age. His favorite team was the Pittsburgh Steelers, and they were always winning back then. My favorite team was the Los Angeles Rams because I liked the ram on the helmet. I also liked the college team Michigan because of the wolverine on their helmets. I was just a kid, and that's how kids choose their teams—colors and helmets.

I changed teams in the '70s. The Houston Oilers drafted Mike Barber as a tight end. He was an All-American player from Louisiana Tech. I was familiar with another player on the team, Earl Campbell, because he was a famous player at that time. I was familiar with Barber because he was from my neck of the woods. The Oilers started rising to the top, and more important to me, they started challenging the team that my brother loved! I started cheering for the Houston Oilers.

Mike Barber was a tough player. He would point his finger at people and let 'em know that he was going to come get them. I liked that kind of stuff, so I started liking Mike Barber more and more.

The Oilers and the Steelers played each other twice in the regular season, and they met in the postseason several times. The games were always pretty epic. It was fun to finally be pulling for a team that could compete with my brother's team. Mike Barber became my favorite player, and I continued to follow him when he was traded to the St. Louis Rams, and then again to the Denver Broncos, retiring in 1985. Whatever team Mike Barber was on became my team to cheer for.

I don't know how many people can say this about their celebrity hero, but I met the man in person in 2001, when I was in prison. Up until this time, I had only ever seen him on TV, but I would know if I had seen him in person because I had seen him with his helmet off during post-game talks, at the national anthem, and during other times they would point the camera at top players in the NFL. I knew what he looked like.

I played offensive tackle and was the head coach of my team. Football in Angola was actually quite a big deal. We had an entire season, with six teams that played. Three teams make the playoffs—the team with the best record gets a bye, and the other top two teams play each other for a spot in the Crunch Bowl. At Louisiana State Penitentiary, the Crunch Bowl was the equivalent to the Super Bowl or the College National Championship game. My team won a spot in the Crunch Bowl, and we went on to play the heavily favored, five-time reigning champions, the East Yard Raiders.

We had to come to their field to play, and to get there, you had to walk through a long walkway—about the length of three football fields. There were forty men on my team, and we had about that many or more spectators with us. We started chanting the whole way there. I was leading the chant, and as we got closer to the Raider's field, I saw a guy with a very familiar face. I told my wide receiver to take over the chant so I could walk up in front of the team and get closer to the familiar face.

"Are you Mike Barber?" I asked.

"Yeah, bud. How are you?" Mike Barber shook my hand. I looked across the field and saw Mike's former head coach, Bum Phillips—one of the most popular coaches in NFL history.

"Is that Bum Phillips?" I asked Mike.

"Yeah. We come to see y'all play the game."

This was the first time I had ever seen my football hero, and I was in prison. I was a nervous wreck as we marched down the field. I started strapping on my shoulder pads, and as I was looking at him, I told the team that Mike Barber and Bum Phillips were there to watch us play football. We prayed as a team, and the two came out for the coin toss. We received the ball. As we went back to our sidelines, Bum walked across the field with the Raiders, and Mike stayed with our team.

Now I was even more of a basket case. The first play of the game I had jumped offsides.

It was a good game with a big crowd on both sidelines. There were probably three or four hundred inmates, security wardens, the head warden, and all sorts of people there for the championship game. We had a 7-6 lead with seconds to go in the game, and the Raiders only had about a yard to go to make another first down. They were inside the twenty, but they didn't have a field goal kicker, so they had to try and blow a hole wide open. A guy named White Lightning on our team didn't let that happen, and the Raiders came up short of the first down.

We took the ball, took a knee, and won our first championship. And I did it in front of my childhood sports hero.

We ended up connecting at that game, and Mike ended up coming to Angola every so often, bringing football equipment, leading a football camp, and even bringing in NFL players. He also brought in famous ministers and ministries into the prison. Since he was the head of Mike Barber Ministries, and I was the senior pastor in Camp C, we had a lot more in common than our love of football. We had a common love for Jesus.

Mike came to the prison three or four times a year. He also invited me to call him any time I wanted to while incarcerated. We became really close.

When Mike was an all-American at twenty-three years old, I was only eleven. When he was in the NFL, I was a teenager. When I was in high school playing defensive end in football, I would fashion myself like Mike Barber. It felt like I knew him long before I ever met him, but once I met him, he became far more than my football hero.

He acted as my pastor, a father figure, a big brother. Sometimes he was the schoolteacher or professor if you will. I accepted him in all of those roles because our friendship while I was incarcerated became more of a spiritual journey. I heard him speak for a group once, and he talked about integrity and maintaining who you are in Christ regardless as to what it looks like around you or what it feels like to you. It's all about your relationship with Christ.

Mike has been in ministry for over forty years. He started his football and prison work towards the end of his career in the NFL. As a matter of fact, he led Coach Bum Phillips to Jesus.

Years after we had met, Mike called and told me he was coming into the prison to film a short birthday film for Jesse Duplantis. Jesse is a rather famous preacher and the founder of Jesse Duplantis Ministries. Mike asked me to get a few guys that I knew who were saved and living for Jesus to make this film. So there were about six of us from prison and a few guys that Mike brought in from the outside to do this special video for Jesse. At least I thought it was supposed to be for Jesse.

Mike's son was there, and he pulled me aside. "When you give your talk on the video, get my dad good," he said. He wanted to play a joke on his dad.

I didn't want to do that in this video for Jesse. Everyone else was saying nice things, and then I was going to be the last speaker.

"Hey, Jesse. I'm glad for you, and I thank you for all of your time coming in and ministering to us. I pray that God blesses you and that you prosper." When I got through, the camera man said, "good job," but he didn't turn the camera off. Mike Barber came up and started to share.

"Hey, Jesse, this is Mike. You know that guy that just spoke before me, the last guy you saw. Well, I thought you should know that he is a pastor here. He is a good friend of mine, and he really is one of the best of the best. But here's the truth—he don't know who he is. You see, he has been a crossdresser for thirty years. He's a she-he."

Everyone in that room was completely cracking up. I just couldn't. My jaw dropped. "Mike! What have you done, man? They gonna show this video at church!"

Mike was laughing uncontrollably. This wasn't the first or last time he would play a prank on me like that. He'd do it in front of one person or 100 people—it didn't matter. He'd start off by telling this story about a man he met through his prison ministry (talking about me) and share my successes, then go on to say something about how I was having trouble leaving some parts of my past behind me—like crossdressing, being the pole man, you name it, nothing was off limits for him when it came to cracking a joke at my expense.

I love Mike Barber. He's a realist, and he's going to tell you what says the Lord whether you like it or not. Everybody needs people like that in their life.

I was about to learn just how much I needed Mike in my life.

Chapter Fifteen

The Hope of Freedom

My sentence was a life sentence without the possibility of parole. Throughout my years of incarceration, I tried to appeal my case before the court, looking for ways that I could become parole eligible. I searched for errors in my case files, looked for things that were said that should not have been said. If there was any reason whatsoever that I could find documentation that my case was not handled correctly, I was going to find it. I did this year after year until the fourth year of filing—I was told that I was barred from pleading my case. There were just no errors to be found.

Knowing that I would die in prison did not keep me from serving God while I was there. My personal record on the inside was stellar. I helped people get their GED, and after four months of teaching, I became the principal of the school. The school I taught at had the highest rate of passing the GED exam on the first try. I just kept on pastoring, playing football, teaching school, and doing my time.

Every five years I was allowed to petition the board and ask for a hearing. If granted a hearing, I would plead my case and ask for parole. The board has the authority to grant or deny the hearing. I was used to being denied. But in 2013, I had Mike Barber on my side.

Mike Barber really stuck by me throughout the years. He believed in me, and he believed that I should be a free man. So much so that he petitioned the governor of Louisiana on my behalf.

Mike went to the governor and plead my case. He told the governor of all the good I was doing on the inside of prison. Late that same night, I was called into the chapel. Mike was there waiting for me.

"Listen buddy, I don't know what we are going to do with your governor. I just went to see him, and you aren't getting a hearing." Mike was visibly upset.

It just wasn't my time.

But Mike did not stop trying to get me out of prison. My next chance came five years later in 2018. I filed my paperwork asking to go before the board, praying they would give me the chance to go before them and ask for a pardon. It was September when I filed the paperwork, and I was praying, asking God to give me a date before the end of the year. In His goodness, He gave me what I asked for—on December 23, 2019, I would go before the pardon board and ask to be parole eligible.

Five people sat on the board and heard my case. I had to get four of them to agree to drop the life sentence and give me parole. Mike Barber was there, and he spoke on my behalf.

"I've been in prisons all over this country, speaking and serving. Let me tell you, this guy is the best of the best. We have planned for him to come and live with us, and he has a job working in my ministry. I trust him so much that I wouldn't hesitate one bit to leave Reginald alone in my house with my wife there."

I had a sheriff who worked in the parish speak on my behalf. When he was done, a lady on the board who knew the sherriff noted that she had never heard him speak at a hearing on behalf of an inmate. His testimony about me was just one more way that God was showing me favor, and He wasn't done yet.

At the hearing, the parole board also listens to the opposition. One person was present in opposition. The Madame Chair called his name, and when he appeared, he gave his statement:

"I have nothing to say. Nothing." And he walked out.

We all cried. Me, Mike Barber, the sheriff, we all cried. I knew that I would get to go home. All five board members agreed to drop the life sentence and make me eligible for parole.

July 7, 2020, the governor of Louisiana signed the papers to grant me parole.

On September 28, 2020, with the warden and the sheriff holding the doors open for me, I walked out of prison as a free man.

PART THREE

Embracing Second Chances

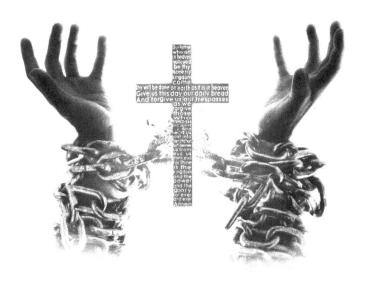

PART THREE

Embracing
Second Chances

Chapter Sixteen

The Call

I was fifty-five when I walked out of the prison doors, and I had a whole new life ahead of me.

I have a four-year accredited degree in Christian ministry, which I obtained while in prison, and I was going to put that degree, along with my personal experience as a prisoner and a pastor to good use with Mike Barber Ministries. Mike's ministry is to go into prisons and minister to the inmates and their families. He offered me a salaried position and a place to stay. To be on the other side—the free man's side—of a ministry like this left me with no doubt that this opportunity was an open door directly from God.

Once I got on my feet financially, my plan was to open up a business with my brother where we would make and sell our rocking chairs and woodworking crafts.

And if Barbara would have me as her husband, I was going to marry that woman.

I had all the hope in the world.

When I walked out, Mike was there to meet me. Barbara wanted to come, but it was already planned that Mike would come get me and take me to Texas. It was about a five-hour drive from Louisiana to Houston, and right around two hours into the drive, Mike's phone rang. It was my former warden at Angola. Now he was a commissioner of prisons in Mississippi—Commissioner Cain.

"Hey Mike, I heard you got your main man Watts out of jail," I could hear Cain through the speakers in Mike's truck. This in itself was mind boggling that I could talk on the phone through the car radio speakers.

Cain went on: "Reg, man, I need you. I need you to come to Mississippi and be a chaplain in the jail. We need to turn Parchman into what Angola was."

"Oh no, no! Man, don't you understand? I just got out."

"Watts, I need you to help me change the culture here. I need you, and Jesus needs you."

I had absolutely no intentions of going back to prison, even as a free man. Even though I was going into prison ministry with Mike, I wouldn't be in prison every day. I would be going into schools and churches too. When Cain started talking about me going to work in prison, I told him that I just couldn't do it.

"I tell you what," I told him on that phone call just two hours after being set free from prison, "Because I love you like a brother and father figure, I'll call on my prayer warriors and get back to you." I told him I needed a few days, so of course, he called me back the next day.

I just needed one person who I trusted to say no.

But no one did. The people I did hear back from told me to go. My brother told me that he saw how God was moving in my life and that I got to make my move for Him. Barbara was the last one. If Barbara said no, then it wouldn't matter what everyone else said, I would listen to her.

"Babe," she said, "God wants you to go to Mississippi." My heart hit the floor. Everybody was telling me the same thing, using different words: "Go to Mississippi."

I accepted the job. I wasn't excited about it, but I knew that it was what God wanted from me.

The weekend before I was to start my new job as chaplain, Mike took me to a Louisiana Tech football game. We stayed overnight in a country club. He pretty much spoiled me. Knowing that I wasn't too excited about moving to Mississippi and working in a prison, Mike told me that no matter what, I always had a job with him and a place to stay.

"Here's what we're gonna do. If you get there and decide in three hours, three days, or three years that you don't want to do this, I'll come get you."

Everything involving the prison system moves slow. Except for this. On Monday, October 22, 2020, Mike dropped me off at the doors of Mississippi State Penitentiary at Parchman where I was officially on payroll. I entered these prison doors as a free man, just twenty-four days after walking out of Angola.

Chapter Seventeen

The Heart of Parchman

Mississippi was never on my radar before I entered Parchman. It's one of the poorest states in our country, and for that reason, some of the staff members who weren't ex-cons felt threatened, even though our jobs weren't taking anything away from what they do, and even though the prison is extremely short staffed. There were a handful of us who had done time at Angola and were now employed by Parchman.

The head chaplain at Parchman was from Angola, along with a maintenance man and a few other chaplains besides me. I got asked all the time, "Are you one of those dudes from Angola?" Word got out that I was another one of Commissioner Cain's guys from Angola.

Early on, one of the staff members called me an inmate in front of a whole bunch of people. It took everything that the Holy Spirit had in me not to respond the way that my flesh wanted to. I didn't know until about a year later, after she got to know me, that she admitted she had been afraid of me. Because I had a life sentence without parole, she assumed I was convicted of rape, murder, or something extremely violent. Over time, I had the opportunity to share my story of getting hooked on crack cocaine and straying away from how my mother raised me.

"I've never killed anyone," I told her. "But that don't make me any better than anybody else."

To most people, I became one of the "guys from Angola." People wanted to know our stories, and we had plenty of opportunities to tell them. I would walk into a dormitory, and somebody would hear me talking and say, "You got an accent. You one of those guys from Angola?" We started to win people over. There were some, both staff and inmates, who thought we were stupid for coming back to work at a prison after being released.

I'm pretty good at administering the word of God without talking about the Bible as much as some people do. I can do this by listening first. Inmates don't get listened to enough. They get talked at all the time by security, by their family, by friends. So I learned early on that my greatest tools were my ears. And not everyone wants to hear a sermon, they want to see a sermon. The only church people some of these inmates will ever see is going to be me and my lifestyle. Most have been burned by the church. They might believe in God, but they can't get any nourishment because they have no desire to fellowship or read the Bible. But I see them look at me while I'm at work and I'm reading my Bible on my break. They see that I'm the nicest person there. They see me sharing my lunch with a person who they know is a drug addict, alcoholic, or doesn't ever bring lunch to work.

Some of the people in prison on both sides of freedom are watching because they want to see you break. So they can say, "That's why I don't serve God right there." I have the opportunity as a chaplain to show people God and to show them hope.

Us chaplains often say we are where we are so that we can show these inmates hope. We are hope stories. People don't get probation, parole, or suspension of a life sentence because when you get life in Louisiana, you got life. Life meant you would die there.

I watched my first Super Bowl out of prison in the dormitory with the inmates, and they couldn't believe I was staying. One guy popped up and started talking to me. He must have been one of the gang leaders because when he started talking, everybody else got quiet.

"Man, you going to watch the Super Bowl here with us?"

"Yeah, I'm going to watch half here and half at unit twenty-five."

Right away I worried if I was making the inmates uncomfortable. Maybe I was keeping some of them from doing their drugs. Maybe I should act like I forgot to do something and leave.

Next thing I knew, guys were coming up to me, bringing me chips, candy bars, a cold drink . . . I had to stop them. They were so taken aback by this chaplain who could be sitting anywhere watching the Super Bowl but chose to watch it with them. We spent the whole game talking about the sport, the last five teams who won the

Super Bowl, what team we wanted to win. It was like for a moment, we weren't in jail, I wasn't a chaplain, and they weren't inmates. We were just a bunch of guys watching the big game. When it was time for me to go, I had guys hugging me on my way out.

The inmates are not used to staff caring, one way or the other. God brought me back to prison so I could show them that someone does care. And it isn't just me, it's God.

Chapter Eighteen

Prison of Prayer

Parchman is about seventy to eighty years behind its time. The conditions, the staff, and the attitude on my first day there all showed it. Parchman is the home to some of the worst of the worst, and the whole prison breeds failure. And change needs to happen on both sides of the line of freedom—with the inmates and the staff. Prison will always remain prison, but there is definitely room for change. I understood right away why Commissioner Cain and God both wanted me there.

I work as a chaplain and as the director of programming at Mississippi State Penitentiary at Parchman. When people ask me what I need to minister well and create a culture of change, I say the same thing—prayer.

My vision is for Parchman to be a prison of prayer. I want to see staff members starting each shift in prayer. I want to see inmates turn to God to handle their battles. I want outside ministries who come into the prison to have prayer for Parchman at the forefront of their minds. A bunch of chaplains who are ex-cons aren't going to change the prison. The commissioner isn't going to change it. It's prayer.

I've seen it happen in my days as an inmate at the bloodiest prison in America. I saw born killers in situations where they would normally hurt somebody just get up and walk away. And it made guys that followed them take that stance as well. I would sit on the edge of a bed with the most violent of offenders who walked away from a fight and listen to him tell me that his days of jugging people with a knife or any other means were over. And I was there long enough to see that he meant it.

I'm here at Parchman to proclaim hope. Whenever I get the opportunity to share my story, people here listen. And there is a level of respect between the inmates and myself because it wasn't that long ago that I was in their shoes.

When a staff member or security officer walks into a zone, there is usually a gang member close by who will shout "Zone! Zone! Zone!" That is a cue to the other inmates on this tier that the police or an administrator is coming in. I got them to stop doing this with me and instead shout "Chaplain on the zone!" It's a whole new level of respect for them to change up their code for me. I explained that I wasn't coming in there to look for drugs or see what they were doing wrong. If I see a weapon, I'll take it without taking an ID or a bed number. I just want the weapon. If they don't hand over their weapons, that's when I bring the heat.

Initially us chaplains who are ex-cons were not welcomed by the staff. They couldn't see past the fact that we were ex-cons. I made a point to see each person at Parchman—inmate or staff member—for what they are, children of God. Barbara and I have cooked for inmates and security who work in visitation. We've been able to feed every department in prison through donations that have come in from the outside. Barbara is good at picking up things from the store when they go on sale. We feed people whenever we have the opportunity to do so.

I've seen the narrative shift from "us versus them," and people are starting to do their jobs. But it's a slow process. There is a lot of money to be made bringing drugs into the prison. A security officer who makes $20 an hour can bring in an extra $5,000 a week in cash by bringing drugs into prison. Gangs on the outside have money to pay to make sure drugs get moved or their son or brother doesn't get hurt. We probably lose one or two security officers a month who are caught bringing in drugs.

But we are winning souls for Christ in the staff members and administration too. The vision I have for Parchman becoming a praying prison, as opposed to a preying prison, is catching on. We have multiple inmate-run churches and other ministries coming in. The prisoners and staff have every chance to hear the gospel. If we can change the way one man feels about God, then we can get two. Each one can reach one. And I know that with every person we bring to the Lord, there's rejoicing in heaven. God is attentive to our cry.

I get messages all the time from people who work here asking me to pray for them. I always do, but I give them an assignment too. Since they believe in the power of prayer, I ask them to pray for something as well. More and more when I cross paths with someone, I'll hear how God is answering their prayer requests.

I'd like to see a group gathering for prayer at every shift change. Every time someone shows up for work, there are some announcements and assignments based on who showed up. It's my desire to see a staff or chaplain-led prayer each time.

I also pray that the security won't look at the inmate as an enemy, and the inmate won't look at security as the enemy. A lot of times inmates will come up to me and ask me to talk to security on their behalf. I preach that security's not the enemy, and if you are not violating, then there should be no fear.

On the outside, it all seems like an impossible task to create a culture of change like this at Parchman. But God showed me in my time at Angola, and through my own life, that nothing is impossible for Him.

Chapter Nineteen

Love Beyond Bars

Barbara was my best friend when I was in prison and my best friend when I was released. Once I found out that I was going to be a free man, the wheels started turning on how I wanted to make this wonderful woman my wife. Barbara is not a one-of-a-million kind of girl, but a one-in-a-lifetime kind of woman.

I had been incarcerated for thirty-one-and-a-half years, over half of my life. I didn't even want to think about marriage while I was in jail. I saw the pain that came with couples who were married and incarcerated. It isn't healthy for a relationship. The burden falls heavily on the person who is not incarcerated because they have to travel, buy the food, put money into her husband's account. You have to be a really strong person, and more often than not, marriages with those who have no possibility of parole do not last.

In June of 2022, Barbara and I went back to New Orleans for my nephew's wedding. I had a ring, and I wanted to take the opportunity to propose while the family was all around. We were in the house that I grew up in, and Barbara was in the kitchen cooking. My brother turned the music on in the living room and had everyone start dancing. His plan was that he was going to ask Barbara to come out to the living room to dance. She followed him, and just as they were about to turn, she saw me down on one knee. It took her a few seconds to figure out what was going on.

"Barbara Morgan, you can make me the happiest man on earth if you tell me you'll marry me. Will you marry me?"

She said yes.

And I was, in fact, the happiest man on the planet.

Four months later we tied the knot.

It was such a beautiful day, a beautiful moment in time. I stood in front of the room with my groomsmen, the bridesmaids, and my good friend, mentor, and officiant, Mike Barber. The doors in the back of the venue opened, and my beautiful bride walked into the room towards me.

Towards me!

I can't even describe the overwhelming awe of the moment when I first saw her. I dropped my head and cried. *My God in heaven, how can you be so so good to me? To give me a bride like Barbara. My soulmate.*

As she neared the front of the room, I wiped the tears from my eyes and took her by the hand. We vowed before God, our friends, and our family to love, honor, and keep each other until heaven takes us home. We sealed that promise with a kiss and danced the night away.

I probably knew that I loved Barbara the first moment I saw her. But for over ten years, we kept our friendship pure.

In His infinite wisdom and kindness, God allowed me to be free from the chains of addiction and prison. Free to love this woman the way Christ loves His church, for the rest of my life.

Chapter Twenty

The Legacy Continues

In 2005 Hurricane Katrina devastated the city of New Orleans. Angola ended up taking in hundreds of inmates from other parishes that were flooded and damaged due to the hurricane. We fed them and ministered to them. It's almost unbelievable to say this, but Angola, one of the bloodiest prisons in America, became a refuge for people from all over Louisiana.

A lady from a local Episcopalian church volunteered to stay on and help with the relief efforts in our prison. She ended up hearing my story as I was sharing with the inmates coming in. The next day she came up to me and insisted that I write a book.

"You gotta write a book. You got to include Angola being a safe haven for all these people. You got to tell your story."

I didn't give her request much thought, but it stayed with me. Every now and then, God would send another person on my path who would say that I should write a book. I heard that over and over, but any attempt to write anything down didn't get me past the first page.

When I was finally released from prison, I heard it even more: *You gotta write a book*. But all of my time was taken up with the work.

But God.

Again. And always.

God has always shown up for me. In every single impossible situation I've ever been in, God was there.

When I was shot and nearly killed, God saved my life.

When I should have been dead on the streets due to an overdose, God saved my life.

When I should have died at the hands of a Colombian gang, God saved my life.

When I was sentenced to life in prison, I accepted Christ into my heart, and He saved my life.

When I should have spent every day of my life in prison and died there, God set me free.

When I was given the opportunity to work with Mike Barber Ministries, God showed me that he had a different plan.

When Barbara came into my life, who would have thought that an ex-con and a retired police officer would find love and marry? God did.

When I needed some help writing this book, God brought the right person and publisher to me.

My story is full of pain, but it is also full of joy. I've seen firsthand Romans 8:28 manifest in front of my very own eyes. That God could take all things—all of my pain, struggles, addiction, and incarceration—and use it for His good and glory. I am amazed just thinking about it.

My story is more than just my own. It's God's story in and through my life.

I get to share my story and all of my experiences, good and bad, to bring hope and freedom to others who are currently incarcerated, and to those who are bound by the chains of their own doing.

Parchman might be a dangerous prison, but it is currently making history. Mississippi is the first state in the country to hire ex-cons who are still on parole back to a prison to work. And it is successful.

My job as a prison chaplain was hard. I've since been promoted to program director at Parchman, and that comes with its own set of hardships. I still do all the things I did as a chaplain—deal with gang activity and deliver death messages every day. I minister to men who experienced unthinkable circumstances when they grew up.

As the program director, I bring in new educational and vocational programs, sports programs—anything that can enhance the life of the prisoner. I also oversee the chaplain ministries. If it sounds like I am spread too thin, you are right. But that is how it is in the prison system. I'm learning how to delegate, and I'm learning the art of putting my foot down, just like my mama and daddy did with us kids. There are times when you have to put your foot down with a little shake to the front of your foot, and there are times when you put it down so gently, others don't even know that your foot has come down on them. In this new position, I have to do both on the daily.

I'm also mindful that I have surpassed some of the employees who have been at Parchman for twenty or more years. Not in salary, but in position. When the job became vacant, I really didn't want it. But I was asked, so I turned to God and asked Him.

Here I am, three years and two months out of prison, and serving as program director at Parchman. I don't know if God will have me stay here forever, or what His plans are for me. But for now, I know I'm right where He wants me to be, serving those he has placed in front of me. I count it all joy that I get to share how God brought me from the chains of sin, to the cross of Christ.

I'm very proud of my time in jail. It took prison for God to get ahold of my heart. If I was never incarcerated, it would have taken a lot longer for me to see, know, and love Jesus. I might have died in my sin. But I didn't. I praise God that he allowed me to serve my sentence.

God showed me that I was free long before I was ever released from prison. Experiencing freedom from sin, freedom from addiction, and freedom in Christ means more to me than the day I walked out of prison.

Epilogue

By Barbara Morgan Watts

When I first met Reginald, I never dreamed we would one day be husband and wife. I never dreamed it, never thought about it, and quite honestly, it is something that never even crossed my mind. Reginald was an inmate at Angola, a prisoner for the rest of his life.

I was no stranger to Angola or the criminal justice system. My work as a juvenile detective and the prison ministry I was involved in through my church brought me to Angola often. Reginald was often cooking in the visitor's shed when I visited with other inmates. When I was first introduced to him, I thought he was a pleasant person. Through a mutual connection on the inside of Angola, I got to be actively involved in helping Reginald sell his hobby craft. It infuriated me to learn that others who said they would help him would actually just take his merchandise and never send him the money for that.

Our visits became regular occasions over the course of ten years. We would talk about anything and everything. I was able to share some of the hurt that I had gone through, and he was able to share the same with me. He was a very easy person to talk to, and I think he felt the same about me. He shared how he carried a lot of guilt over the pain he had caused his family, particularly his mother, even after being raised in a loving home. Our friendship came easy for both of us.

Ten years into our friendship, he shared that he had true feelings for me. I was completely blown away. I knew his ups and his downs. I knew when he needed encouragement as a pastor, and I knew when he needed encouragement as an inmate. I often prayed to God to allow me to be the person to help Reginald in his own spiritual journey. I prayed that I would have the spirit to be in tune with what he was going through even though he was incarcerated, and I was free. I really thought I would have known if he had feelings for me beyond friendship. But I didn't.

After Reginald shared his feelings with me, letting me know that he wanted to marry me, I again went to God in prayer. God said yes, and so did I.

It is one of the greatest joys of my life that God has allowed me to witness the work of God in Reginald's life, both behind bars and beyond them. He was incarcerated for thirty-one years and then went back into prison as a free man so that others on the inside can see the same hope that Reginald had while he was behind bars. It is so amazing for me to see the level of respect and thanks the offenders give to Reginald. He tells the inmates all the time, "If God did it for me, He can do it for you." Reginald has lived it, and those he ministers to believe it. It is truly a beautiful thing.

I'm no longer taking orders and collecting fees for his hobby craft, but I am taking phone calls for him while he

Epilogue

is working at Parchman. His story is so incredible—he has requests to speak and minister to groups, churches, and other prisons all the time. God's faithfulness through his story has been changing lives. Addiction is a huge stronghold for people in every walk of life. You can go through a twelve-step program and support meetings, but until people know that they need to surrender their addiction to God and sell out to Him, being released from that stronghold is unlikely. Many try but often relapse. God has shown Reginald in a very personal way that until you truly repent and surrender it all to God, then you can't find freedom from your addiction. Reginald should have been dead from an overdose, dead from a gunshot wound, and dead due to his sin. But the God who controls the universe gave freedom to Reginald, even in the most unlikely of places—prison.

And if God can conquer death, there is nothing our almighty Creator cannot do. What God has done for us, we could never do ourselves. When people hear and read Reginald's story, I want them to know that there is no limit to what God can do. He is merciful and loving, and no matter how many times we mess up, we can always go back to Him. His arms are always open, His ears are always kind. He's never too busy.

He wasn't too busy for a Louisiana man who was caught up in addiction, criminal activity, and—by every account of man and the law—was due to spend the rest of his earthly days behind bars.

He's not too busy for you.

Acknowledgements

I wanted to take a moment to mention some of the people who have been instrumental in my life.

To my wife and best friend, you inspired me through it all . . . there is no me without you.

To my daughter, Taylor C. Watts, you are and have always been my motivation.

To my parents, the late Robert and Lillie Mae Watts, with little, you did so much for so many.

To my oldest brother Kelvin, I love you more than you know. Thanks for never turning your back on me . . . no matter what.

To my brother, Rob, you have always taken care of me, stood up for me, and fought for me. It blesses my heart and brings me great strength to know that you believe in me.

To my Aunt and Godmother, Beverly, you are the leader of the pack.

To Mike and Shahein Barber, thank you for all that you did, do, and will do, because you trusted me.

Adonis Brooks, you are like the little brother I never had. Brian Ditrich, you were my first true friend at Angola. Dkystra, the Mexican drummer and true friend. Pastor Sidney Deloch, a gospel-ready trendsetter. Todd Jackson and Armand June, my life-long best friends. Mark St. Julian, a humble teddy-bear who kept me laughing when I wanted to cry. Ulysses Jones always keeps it real. Pastor Daryl Waters, a quiet storm.

Warden Burl Cain, you are a true pioneer. You opened the doors in the system for bringing Bible college into prisons, and then allowing ex-cons like me to work as free men in prisons. Ron Olivier (Teirsen and Ra-Re), George King, and Maurice Clifton, you were all the first to do it—and gave me the courage to follow.

To Tapas Sarma (with a hearty push from Mrs. Chanel)—thank you for dedicating yourself to make sure I stayed on the straight a narrow.

To Big Dan Stratton and Faith Exchange Church—thank you for being the muscle I needed.

To the Camp C church and football team—because of you, I learned about leadership and discipline.

To Mama Morgan, I can never express how much I love you. Thank you for loving me and imparting wisdom in my life. Scott and Casey Clarkson, our bonus family and dancing partners, you are the trendsetters for what security is supposed to look like. The sheriff, Steven McCain, and people of Grant Parish, you are all people of love.

Jack and Teni Tillery, you always believed in me. Kevin and Carmen Miller, my brother and sister, the real dynamic duo. Danny and Joyce Pauley, true servants to the needy. The people of Moss Bluffs, you have all been so helpful.

Epilogue

Bishop Mac Lee, a weeping prophet. Bishop Roderick Mitchell, a great teacher. Pastor Rusty and Anne Griffin, thank you for the wisdom you imparted. Pastor Dan and Anne Straton, lovers of our souls.

Aunt Barbara Freeman, you make us laugh. Dion Hills, you are a breath of fresh air.

To the late George Spears, you taught me more about pastoring than anyone on this earth. Manny and Barbara Mills, all I can say is "ALELUYAA-ALELUYA!!!"

My nephews, Leo, KJ, Tank, Ace, Deuce, Tré, and Five, you all have kept me rolling.

To my nieces, Keta, Kenedra, Ashley, Kaneta, Amber, Qua, and so many others to name, but you all lift my spirit.

To all other family members, I love you all.

The O'havers, with such a sweet spirit, you have made my transition easier.

To the countless people whose support, encouragement, and contributions have shaped my journey through incarceration and beyond, I am profoundly grateful. While it is impossible to mention everyone by name, please know that your kindness and assistance have not gone unnoticed. I thank you and I keep you in my prayers.

In Christ,
Reginald D. Watts

About the Authors

Reginald D. Watts, Program Director at Mississippi State Penitentiary at Parchman, is a living testament to the power of faith, and resilience. Having experienced the depths of addiction firsthand, Reginald understands the challenges many face within the grip of substance abuse and incarceration. His own journey took a remarkable turn when he found strength in his faith, leading him to overcome addiction and eventually receive a miraculous pardon from a life sentence at Angola State Penitentiary.

Today, Reginald is deeply committed to making a positive difference in the lives of those within the incarcerated community. He works to provide guidance, support, and opportunities for rehabilitation, believing wholeheartedly in the potential for transformation, even in the most challenging circumstances.

In addition to his role within the correctional system, Reginald is a passionate speaker who travels to churches and prisons across the country, sharing a message of hope and redemption. He is a vital part of Mike Barber Ministries, an organization dedicated to serving the incarcerated community and fostering positive change in neighborhoods, cities, and beyond. With a mission rooted in faith and compassion, Mike Barber Ministries seeks to break the cycle of incarceration by offering hope, healing, and restoration through the transformative power of Jesus Christ.

Reginald and his wife, Barbara, are committed to serving and inspiring others, demonstrating that, with faith, lives can be changed.

Follow Reginald on:
◎ @reginald.watts.988
❙ @ReginaldWatts
✉ rd3000watts@gmail.com

About the Authors

Robin Grunder is an experienced journalist, author, and highly sought-after ghostwriter. She is currently the executive editor of Legacy Press Books. She is a regular speaker on the topic of legacy writing, memoir, and self-publishing your life-story at writers' conferences around the country.

Some of her writing credits include pieces in *Chicken Soup for the Soul*, regional and national parenting publications, regional newspapers, and several ghostwritten books. Most recently, Robin has written and published *Memoir in the Margins of Psalms, Journaling Your Life-Story in the Margins of God's Story*.

Robin and her husband Brian have a blended family of seven adult children and two grandchildren. They make their home in Eastern Iowa.

Visit Robin at www.robingrunder.org
Follow on ⓘ and ⨍: **@RobinGrunderAuthor**